at home with

pictures

at home with

pictures

paige gilchrist

ARRANGING
& DISPLAYING
PHOTOS, ARTWORK
& COLLECTIBLES

LARK BOOKS A DIVISION OF STERLING PUBLISHING CO., INC.
NEW YORK

EDITOR:
PAIGE GILCHRIST

ART DIRECTOR:
CHRIS BRYANT

PHOTOGRAPHY:
WRIGHT CREATIVE
PHOTOGRAPHY & DESIGN

COVER DESIGN:
BARBARA ZARETSKY

COVER PHOTOGRAPHY:
SANDRA STAMBAUGH

ILLUSTRATORS:
OLIVIER ROLLIN
LORELEI BUCKLEY

ASSISTANT EDITOR:
VERONIKA ALICE GUNTER

EDITORIAL ASSISTANTS:
DELORES GOSNELL
MARISA THOMPSON

PRODUCTION ASSISTANTS:
HANNES CHAREN
SHANNON YOKELEY
LORELEI BUCKLEY

SPECIAL PHOTOGRAPHY:
JESSIE WALKER COMPANY

SANOMA SYNDICATION
Alexander van Berge
Mirjam Bleeker
Dennis Brandsma
Frank Brandwijk
John Dummer
Hotze Eisma
Luuk Geertsen
Rene Gonkel
Paul Grootes
Ewout Huibers
Anneke de Leeuw
Louis Lemaire
Eric van Lokven
Otto Polman
Jeroen van der Spek
Hans Zeegers

Library of Congress has cataloged the hardcover edition as follows:

Gilchrist, Paige.
   At home with pictures : arranging & displaying photos,
artwork & collections / Paige Gilchrist.
     p. cm.
   Includes index.
   ISBN 1-57990-360-6
   1. Pictures in interior decoration. 2. Collectibles in interior
decoration. I. Title.
   NK2115.5.P48 G55 2002
   747'.9–dc21   2002069466

10 9 8 7 6 5 4 3 2 1

Published by Lark Books,
a division of Sterling Publishing Co., Inc.
387 Park Avenue South, New York, N.Y. 10016

First Paperback Edition 2004
© 2003, Lark Books

Distributed in Canada by Sterling Publishing,
c/o Canadian Manda Group, One Atlantic Ave., Suite 105
Toronto, Ontario, Canada M6K 3E7

Distributed in the U.K. by Guild of Master Craftsman Publications Ltd.
Castle Place, 166 High Street, Lewes, East Sussex, England BN7 1XU
Tel: (+ 44) 1273 477374, Fax: (+ 44) 1273 478606
Email: pubs@thegmcgroup.com, Web: www.gmcpublications.com

Distributed in Australia by Capricorn Link (Australia) Pty Ltd.
P.O. Box 704, Windsor, NSW 2756 Australia

If you have questions or comments about this book, please contact:
Lark Books • 67 Broadway, Asheville, NC 28801 • (828) 253-0467

Manufactured in China

ISBN 1-57990-360-6 (hardcover) 1-57990-595-1 (paperback)

acknowledgments

ABUNDANT THANKS TO:

■ The tasteful and generous collectors who stripped their walls bare to loan us many of the pictures featured throughout the book: **KATHERINE** and **STEVE AIMONE**, **CHANDLER W. GORDON** and **MIEGAN SMITH GORDON**, **DANA IRWIN**, **MARTHE LE VAN** and **RICK MORRIS**, **SARA** and **GERALD LE VAN**, **CELIA NARANJO**, **CAROL TAYLOR**, and **TERRY TAYLOR**.

■ **CHANDLER** and **MIEGAN GORDON** again, who graciously allowed us to sink our picture hooks into the pristine walls of their **CAPTAIN'S BOOKSHELF**, and Terry Taylor, who actually painted his walls *before* we showed up with hammers and nails, just so we would have a variety of colors to work with.

■ **LINDA WHITTMIRE MATTHEWS**, of **ARTWORKS AND FRAMING**, Asheville, NC, who let us borrow mat and frame samples for various shots.

■ **LIZ WAGGONER**, who generously lent her expertise in buying and placing art during the early planning stages of this book.

■ **KEVIN MILLS**, who took time away from his real job to help us organize, lug, haul, and hang dozens of pictures.

■ **EXPOSURES** (1-800-572-2502, www.exposuresonline.com), a company specializing in picture frames and accessories, who loaned us numerous images. They appear on pages 24, 27, 30, 36, 44, 49–50, 62–63, 71–72, 76, 80, 84, 86–87, 94, 98, 100–101, 107, 112, 121–123, 125, and 128.

■ **GONZALO GALDIZ** at **KOSMOS DESIGNS**, Asheville, NC, for the terrific orange pillows used on the book's cover.

We would also like to recognize the artists whose paintings, photographs, and other works appear in this book:

Steve Aimone
Walter Anderson
Leonard Baskin
Mary Bero
Rich Borge
Evan Bracken
Jeanette DeLisle DeSales
Molly Doctrow
June Glenn
Judy Guyton
Curt Haase
Edward Hopper
Dana Irwin
Clare Leighton
Susan Levi-Goerlich
Sara Le Van
Tom Lundberg
Malaika
Ron Meisner
Joan Miró
Barry Moser
Jean Wall Penland
Jay Pfeil
Joe Quillan
Missy Stevens
Suzanne Stryk
Ariko Sugiyama
A. Kellogg Tyler

contents

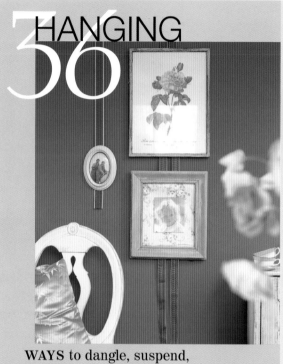
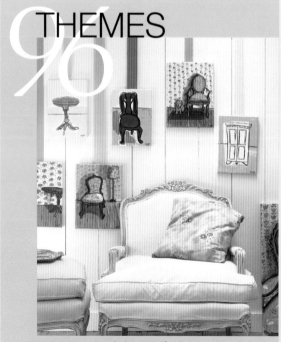
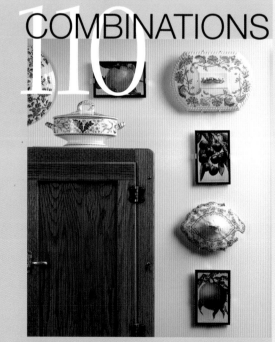

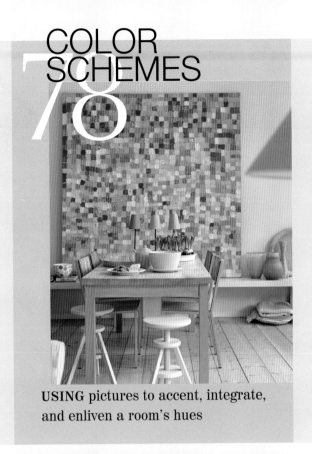
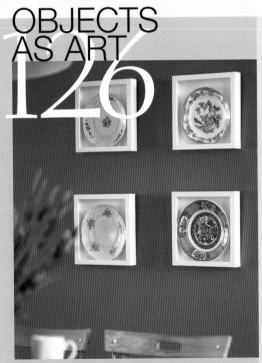

introduction

R ECENTLY, our growing company moved several blocks north to a larger office space in a still-being-renovated warehouse. We all learned a great deal about one another in the process. Some of us are neat and orderly packers, for example, and others simply wind duct tape around open file bins. Some arrange office furniture by moving heavy objects back and forth, others draw detailed floor plans first.

But there's one thing that was true across the board. Even as the movers were still delivering truckloads of office equipment and the carpenters were still hanging doors, people were setting framed photographs of their kids and pets on top of cardboard boxes and propping their favorite paintings on otherwise empty shelves. Days before the phone system was installed, colorful tapestries were hanging on the conference room walls. And a full week before anyone hooked up the photocopier near my office, someone *had* taken the time to mount a small print that fit perfectly in the space above it.

The message was clear. Though pictures may not serve a purpose as practical as a chair or a lamp, they're just as important to people who want to transform a space into a home—even if it's the home away from home where they spend their work days.

Pictures, from photographs, prints, and paintings to mixed-media collages and fabric wall hangings, showcase who we care about and what we find beautiful. They celebrate where we've been, what we've done, and the subjects and styles that strike us as interesting. They also communicate those aspects of us to others. In other words, pictures are part of who we are. So where did we get the idea that hanging them where we like them takes a master's degree in fine arts? Or worse, that if we don't have masterpieces and homes resembling galleries to hang them in, we shouldn't bother?

Arranging and displaying pictures is an art form that's open to all of us. There are a few techniques that make it easier and some general guidelines for getting started, solving problems, and achieving certain looks; we give you an overview of all of them. But decorating with pictures is mostly about experimenting with your own unique puzzle pieces of color, style, space, and shape until you come up with something you like. This book provides more than 100 examples of where that experimenting might lead.

Whether you have a stack of family photographs you can't decide how to display, or empty white walls you're not sure how to fill, we show you how to approach the situation in a variety of ways:

- pairing pictures with the right mats and frames
- using creative hanging techniques
- trying out different wall arrangements
- playing with combinations of color

When it's more a question of *what* to hang, we give you innovative ideas for creating theme displays and assembling combinations that blend pictures with everything from wooden sculptures to childhood memorabilia. Perhaps most helpful of all, we give you permission to broaden your definition of *picture* altogether, with examples of displays featuring antique game boards, painted china, a collection of keys, and other objects ranging from the ordinary to the unusual.

Sprinkled throughout the book, you'll also find problem-solution boxes and clever suggestions for breaking picture-display rules (and getting away with it). There's also a regular feature called *Off the Wall*—ideas for what to do when you don't want to actually *hang* your pictures.

Use the pages that follow as springboards. Use them as sources for new ideas. Most of all, use them as inspiration for the many ways pictures can turn anyplace into one that feels like home.

frames & mats

One of your first **decisions** about displaying any picture is how to set it off. Think of a picture's frame and mat as its attire. Depending on the personality of the picture, the place it will hang, and the statement you want it to make, you can surround it with the equivalent of a feather boa, a tailored suit, a comfy sweatshirt—or nothing at all.

frames

1 Sand it down and paint it a color that matches your rugs.

2 Decoupage it with magazine clippings.

3 Drill holes in it and string on alphabet beads that spell your child's name.

4 Cover it with faux fur.

5 Gild it.

6 Sculpt on it with papier-mâché.

7 Coat it with grout, then embed the grout with small stones or scraps of glazed tile.

8 Use stencils to paint on a design.

9 Pickle it to give it a bleached, weathered patina.

10 Hot-glue boisterous fake flowers all over it.

IN TERMS OF PURE FUNCTION, a frame's job is to define the edges of an image and help it to stand out from the space around it. But the frame you choose—its size, shape, color, texture, material, and weight—can also play a major role in your image's final form. Take something as simple as a postage stamp. Put it in a miniature frame featuring delicate gold filigree, and you have one look. Slip it, instead, into the small opening of a wide-sided frame whose fire-engine color picks up the red flecks in the stamp, and you have a look that's completely different. Whether you're working with a custom framer or fitting your pictures into ready-made frames yourself, you can find styles that range from sporty to serious, whimsical to tried-and-true traditional.

Clip frames are made of plain glass fronts, hardboard backs, and silver clips that hold them together. If you tend to like simple and unadorned, these frames are likely to appeal to your no-nonsense style. Technically, clip frames are clear holders rather than traditional frames, and they're especially suited to more casual pieces, including postcards, posters, and prints.

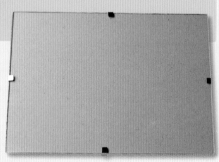

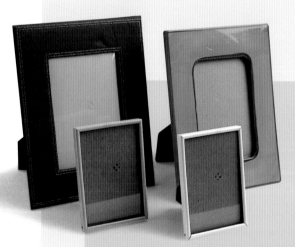

Colored frames can intensify the color in a photograph or painting, help a picture coordinate or contrast with a wall and the surrounding furnishings, or cause a picture to make a splash in an otherwise neutral environment.

Shadow boxes are essentially deep-backed frames that are perfect for displaying three-dimensional works of art as well as other objects, from model ships to handmade puppets. For more of a museum-style look, you can also use display cases made from clear plastic sheeting. The one above right is a four-sided case with a solid back.

Glass shops and well-stocked frame shops also sell five-sided cases, and framers can create customized cases to fit specific pieces.

Wood frames—from plain and untreated to bleached, pickled, color-washed, or richly stained and polished—can complement a wide spectrum of looks, whether you want understated and modern, folksy and rustic, or time-honored and classic.

Corner blocks and other corner details, from raised flowers and leaves to lyres and masks, have been used to add interest to frames for hundreds of years. As in this example, they can also help the frame coordinate with the picture inside.

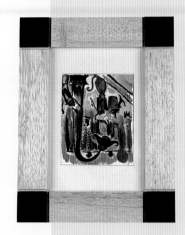

Ornately carved frames that are gilded or painted a rich, deep color provide a heavy, robust outline for everything from oil paintings to family portraits.

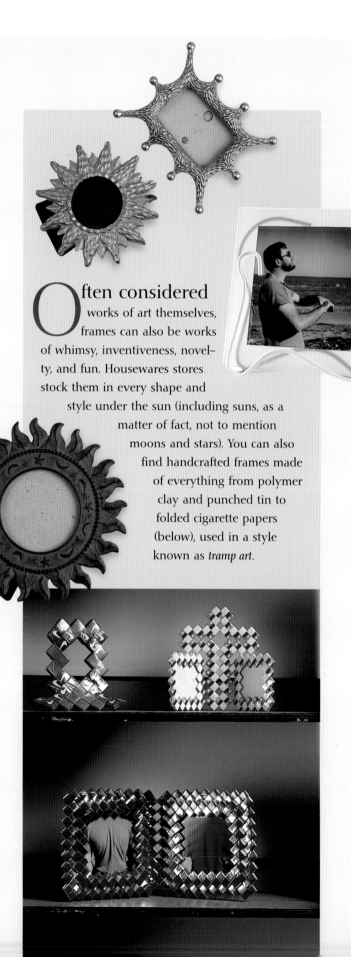

Often considered works of art themselves, frames can also be works of whimsy, inventiveness, novelty, and fun. Housewares stores stock them in every shape and style under the sun (including suns, as a matter of fact, not to mention moons and stars). You can also find handcrafted frames made of everything from polymer clay and punched tin to folded cigarette papers (below), used in a style known as *tramp art*.

There are times when the framing look you want is one of no frame at all. Painted canvases stretched over wooden supports lend themselves especially well to this fresh-from-the-studio style that lets the picture speak for itself.

14

Metal frames are some of the most popular. They're easy to find and affordable, and they give pictures a spare, streamlined border. The mood they create will depend on the finish you choose.

■ Gold frames are classic and warm. In most cases, they create a neutral break between the picture and the wall.

■ Silver or aluminum frames are cool, modern, and especially suited to pure pinks, minty greens, and grays and blues, and they look good setting off abstract works. They also work well with clear, fresh colors, although they can tend to tone down the colors rather than make them pop. Aluminum frames also come in a variety of metallic finishes, from bronze and sepia toned to iridescent blue.

■ Black metal frames give you the sleekest, most chic look of all, especially if you combine them with white or off-white mats and black-and-white photos or other imagery.

frame
profiles

Regardless of a frame's perimeter shape, its sides are contoured in one of three ways.

■ The most common style is for the frame's pieces to slope inward toward the picture. The slight bevel leads the viewer's eyes into the featured image. Landscapes and pictures with lots of detail benefit from inward-sloping frames.

■ Another option is for the frame's pieces to extend out from the picture on a level plane. This style is often effective for setting off modern and minimalist works.

■ Third, a frame's pieces can slant away from the picture, either steeply or through a more gentle curve, making the edge of the frame near the picture more pronounced. An outward-sloping frame is a good choice for still lifes and portraits.

IN ADDITION, though there are many variations on the theme, frames come in one of two general forms. They're either angular and straight-edged (above) or rounded and softer (right).

framing tips

If you plan to hang a picture on a busy wall—maybe one covered with wallpaper that features an intricate design—choose a subtle frame that contrasts strongly with the wall color and design.

Choose a frame that brings out what's interesting to you about your picture rather than one that simply matches your decor. Let the frame help emphasize the picture's drama, reinforce its tranquility, or highlight some other quality.

A dark frame—in this case accompanied by a wide, dark mat—can make any picture more vibrant.

At the same time, play with blending a picture's frame with its setting: a polished wood frame over an antique chest of drawers, a gun-metal gray aluminum frame in a high-tech home office. Matching a frame to its surroundings is more important if you're hanging just a single piece. You'll be more interested in having it make a specific decorative contribution to the room.

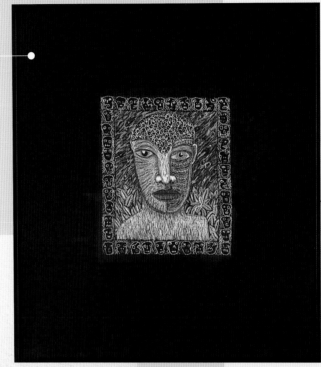

mats

These cardboard pieces help create a contrast—if you want one—between your picture and frame. Using no mat at all, on the other hand, often intensifies the look of whatever you're framing. You can buy mats off the shelf in a variety of standard sizes and colors. Ready-made mats sold at craft and housewares stores come with basic beveled and rectangular openings as well as specialty cuts, from circles to Christmas trees. A professional frame shop can provide you with a wider variety of mat colors, cut non-standard sizes for you, and handle techniques such as layering several mats to create a more elaborate border around a picture.

If you want to punctuate or strengthen the color in a picture, try pairing it with a colored mat.

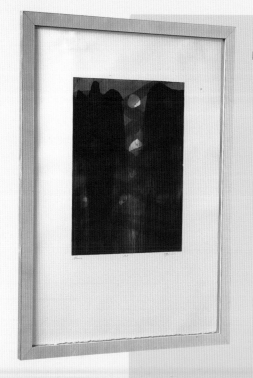

The size and cut of the mat can have a huge effect on how a picture looks. In general, you want any mat to measure at least slightly wider than the width of the frame; if the widths are identical, the effect will be flat and predictable. But beyond that, almost anything goes. The example on the right shows how you can intensify the drama of even a small line drawing by surrounding it with an oversize mat. In the picture on the left, the mat area below the painting is just slightly larger than the area above it, a small variation that gives the overall display an interesting bit of movement.

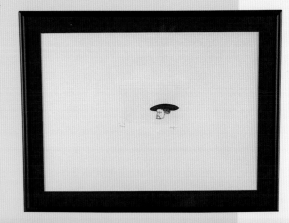

Double mats, also called stepped mats, are created by layering one mat on top of the other, typically revealing only about ¾ inch (1.9 cm) to 1 inch (2.5 cm) of the inner mat. You can use the technique to add depth, draw viewers in, or accentuate a color, as the vibrant strip of yellow mat does here.

FIVE ways to personalize a MAT

1 Cover it with velvet or some other luxurious fabric.

2 Glue on a layer of handmade paper.

3 Stamp it with symbols that coordinate with the picture you're framing.

You can find mats that have been specially treated in a number of ways—wrapped with hand-made paper, saturated with a color wash, marbled, stippled, or covered with fabric, like the ones shown here. All are excellent ways to add subtle texture to a display.

4 Decorate it with rub-on transfers designed especially for mats. They come in motifs ranging from swirls and spirals to all the letters in the alphabet.

Choose a mat cut in a shape other than the standard rectangle or square if it will help set off the contour of your picture. Here, a circle provides the perfect border for a mandala (left), and two long strips of mat help accentuate the long, horizontal shape of a painted crocodile (below).

5 You can find wallpaper today in everything from grass cloth to silk. Cover your mat in a layer of it, attaching it with spray adhesive.

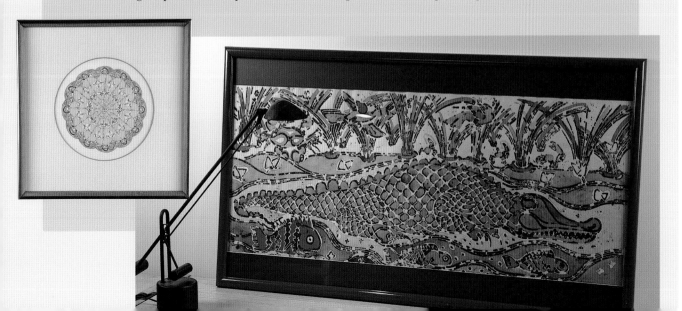

The technical term for omitting the mat altogether is *close framing*. The technique is used most often with oil paintings, which you shouldn't cover with glass, either.

SAFEKEEPING

Others may not consider it fine art. But if you're framing something that's important to you—from your daughter's first finger-painting project to a collection of baseball cards—and you want to protect it from the damaging effects of acidity, heat, and light, here are some extra-care steps you can take.

■ Choose acid-free materials for your mat and the picture's backing, whether you're working with a professional or framing your piece yourself. Acid degrades photographs and other paper-based images. Acid-free materials are typically labeled *conservation quality*, *museum quality*, or *archival quality*.

■ It's best not to store or display valuable or heirloom pictures in rooms such as kitchens and bathrooms, where the temperature and humidity vary a great deal. You also want to avoid displaying them near heat sources, such as radiators, fireplaces, and air ducts. For more information on picture locations, see the sidebar on page 39.

■ Don't hang a display in direct sunlight. Strong light will fade and dry photos and other artwork.

■ For especially valuable pieces, consider ultraviolet-proof thermoplastic (also known as conservation or museum-grade glass). A UV filter on your windows offers the same protection, and positioning pieces under incandescent rather than fluorescent lights helps, too.

SHOP TALK

While buying ready-made mats and frames and fitting your pictures in place yourself is by far the least expensive way to go, there may be times when you'd rather have a professional framer handle the task. Frame shops offer a wider selection of color and style of both mats and frames than do stores that sell premade versions. And a professional framer may be better at handling tricky jobs (such as sewing a painted piece of silk to a mat) or more elaborate styles (maybe layering several custom-cut mats). When you take a picture to a professional framer, here are some additional items and pieces of information it's helpful to have.

■ Paint chips showing the color of the wall the picture is likely to hang on and the colors of nearby walls.

■ Fabric swatches from the room's furniture and accessories. (Or, toss a throw pillow and a couple of prominent accent pieces in a bag and tote them along.)

■ Samples of colors you'd like to use for the mat and/or frame, if you already have some ideas.

■ Size specs on the room where the picture will hang and of the open wall area, so the framer can get an idea of proportion. If possible, bring photos of the space.

putting it all together

Still trying to get a picture of how frames and mats can combine to create totally different looks—or, more to the point, the look you want? Let us show you a few. Here are two examples of how we used off-the-shelf frames and simple matting techniques to set off the same picture several different ways.

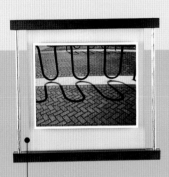

CONTEMPORARY
float frame
no mat
wood and metal supports

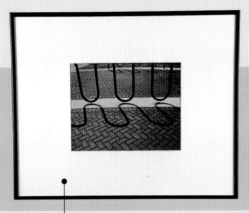

MINIMALIST
no-frills black wooden frame
wide off-white mat

TRADITIONAL
heavy, carved frame
dark mat

SERENE
delicate, brushed-metal frame
soft-colored coordinating mat

MODERN
bleached box frame holding
two sheets of glass
casual matless display

BOLD
stark black frame
eye-popping mat in the
picture's complementary color

Here are two very different looks that illustrate the exact same fact: a frame can help a picture merge seamlessly with its setting. The classic black frame here is a match, not only in terms of its color, which blends soothingly with the surrounding shades of black, white, gray, and the neutral wood color, but also its shape. The frame's sleek, black rectangle mimics the black scaffolding on the nearby doors and the grid pattern on the couch base. What if you wanted the photograph to be the room's focal point instead of just a subtle feature? A warm, pure-yellow frame would do it in this room. So would bright red.

At left, a much more ornate frame settles prettily into place amid the gentle curves of the couch and nearby mirror. Its antiqued surface is identical to the patches of whitewashed and distressed wood in the room, and its small clusters of carved flowers echo the floral fabrics on the pillows just below it.

L ike people, pictures tend to behave differently, depending on how you treat them. Put a small piece, like the photo here, in a thin, subtle frame, and hang it as part of a cluster, and it will blend politely and quietly into the crowd. But position it off by itself in an impressive, over-size frame, and the simplest and sparest of images will happily act as center of attention.

breaking the rules and getting away with it

Traditionally, the bigger the picture, the bigger (as in wider and more substantial) the frame. The opposite is usually the rule for smaller pictures—we're told to pair a tiny picture with a diminutive, delicate frame. In some cases, however, you can use a disproportionally large frame, like the gold- and silver-leaf frames shown here, to draw attention to a petite picture, giving it added presence and importance.

Hints and suggestions are

sometimes better than direct pronouncements. That's true when it comes to picture framing, too. These mitered, glued, and nailed-together twigs nonchalantly imply a frame around a tacked-up piece of handmade paper, rather than form a standard one. For different looks using this basic concept, consider tacked-together strips of lathe, copper pipe connected with elbow joints, or strands of yarn or jute wound around pushpins at the "frame's" four corners.

IF you crave order and balance in your home decor, frames and mats can be a great unifier. These warm, wooden frames and subdued green mats obviously add to the harmony here, blending naturally with their rich wood and green surroundings and echoing the tree images they contain. But they also contribute to the tranquility of the scene by keeping everything symmetrical. The mat openings have been individually cut to accommodate the four different photos, which vary slightly in size. The perimeter measurements of the mats, however, are the same, ensuring that they all fit neatly into a restful arrangement of identically shaped frames.

at home with pictures

Thanks to black mats with customized cuts, each of these pretty botanical etchings is showcased as an individual work of art, while still functioning as part of a classic set. The different-size openings give the display a sense of movement, and the strong black color adds to the graphic appeal of the images.

OFF
the WALL

IF YOU DECIDED TO LEAVE CORKBOARD AND THUMBTACKS BEHIND when you moved out of your college dorm, here's another option. Cover a frame's backing with a remnant of a luxurious fabric—crushed velvet, perhaps, or hand-painted silk. Then use elegant beaded hat pins to hold the pieces of your rotating display in place.

problem
solving

problem: A big, blank wall you'd like to fill with a framed photo or painting. Trouble is, you don't own a massive piece of artwork that can do the job all by itself.

solution: Here are two examples of how frames and mats can turn something as simple and easy to come by as a collection of snapshots into a wall display with visual weight. On the left, a spacious wooden frame with small openings transforms three separate shots into a unified and substantial display. The three stacked frames on the right, hung directly on top of one another, function as a single, vertical work. At the same time, the mats inside, each cut with different openings, showcase a variety of photo sizes and shapes.

IN this sleek,
neutral, patternless room, the eye is left with no question about where it should focus its gaze. When a setting so effectively serves as a backdrop for a single striking image, an elaborate frame might only confuse the issue. Here, thin off-white strips of wooden lathe are all this dramatic painting needs. They finish its edges—and perhaps even play quietly off the same-colored sofa and floor pillows—but never compete for attention.

IF your life is full, varied, and in constant motion, maybe you'd like aspects of your decorating style to reflect all that. This decidedly unchoreographed display, featuring a simply framed piece surrounded by others with no frames at all, gives the impression that just a few days ago (if not a few hours ago), some of the pictures were hanging on a nearby wall, while others were still in a sketchbook. The casual approach to both framing and arranging sets a work-in-progress tone viewers can relax by.

S tart playing around with possibilities for found-object frames, and the line between art and framing device blurs. For this simple installation of batik panels surrounded by an old window frame, the vibrant kitchen wall even fills in as the mat. Like the concept but want something less rustic? Fashion a one-of-kind frame (including cutting out a center opening, when necessary) from something else on this starter list of possibilities:

- Vinyl record
- Wrought-iron back of a bistro chair
- Serving tray
- Frisbee
- Hand mirror

at home with pictures

OFF
the WALL

MAYBE IT'S A NUMBERED ORIGINAL BY A WELL-KNOWN ARTIST. Or maybe it's your five-year-old's masterpiece featuring blue trees and a lime-green sun. Whichever, nothing elevates its importance like displaying it on an easel. An easel also makes your picture's placement flexible. You can move it easily into the center of things, off to the sidelines, or away to a completely different space.

These boxy frames with double panes of glass let images float in space, so the shadows they cast on the wall become a part of the overall display. The effect raises even the most ordinary imagery—snapshots, clippings, or the overlapping postcards shown here—to the status of objets d'art.

hanging

Most of the time, you'll need nothing more than a standard picture hanger and a hammer to install your display on the wall. Occasionally, you'll want a hanger with more strength or a screw and an anchor to better grip your wall. We walk you through all the standard hanging tools and techniques on the next few pages. Then we give you a chapter full of additional ideas, from dangling your pictures from decorated pegs to attaching them to magnetic strips.

hardware
&how to use it

If you want to have several options on hand, buy an inexpensive picture-hanging kit at a craft or hardware store. Here's how to use the pieces from a standard kit.

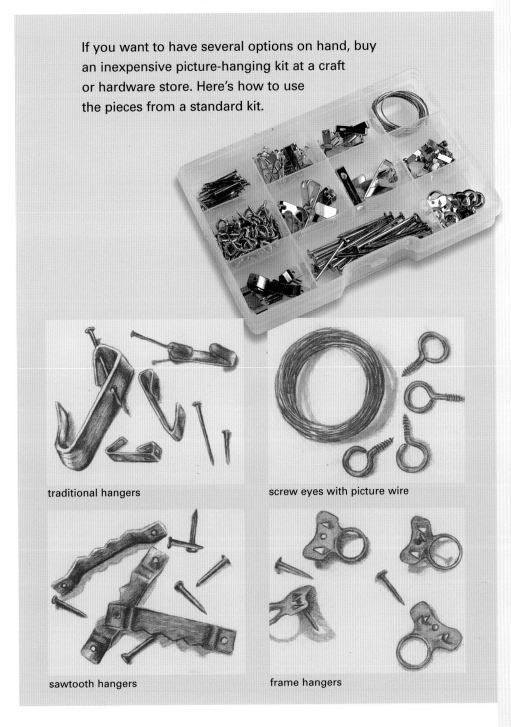

traditional hangers

screw eyes with picture wire

sawtooth hangers

frame hangers

TRADITIONAL HANGERS

They have a nail that runs through the top and a hook that acts as a hanger, and come in various sizes, each with the capacity to hold a specific amount of weight. Picture hangers work in both drywall and plaster, although they can chip plaster. Hangers sold separately as "professional" picture hangers have thin, sharp, hardened nails that are less likely to cause chipping.

SCREW EYES AND PICTURE WIRE

If your picture isn't yet outfitted with a hanging apparatus, this is one option. To position the eyes, measure the height of the frame, and mark pilot holes one-third of the way down. Drill holes slightly smaller than the diameter of the threaded portion of the eyes, then twist the eyes in by hand. Cut a piece of braided wire that measures one and a half times the picture's width. Wrap each end around a screw eye and then around itself. For heavy pictures, run two wires between the screw eyes, and support each with a picture hanger. Space the hangers at least half the picture's width apart.

SAWTOOTH HANGERS AND NAILS

These pieces offer another hanging option, one best suited to very small, light pieces you can hang from a single central point. Nail the hanger into the middle of the back top edge of the frame. Instead of hanging it from a picture hanger, settle the "teeth" of the hanger over a small nail.

FRAME HANGERS

Alternatives to sawtooth hangers, these are for heavier pieces that require hangers on both sides to keep them level. Attach one to each of the back top corners of the frame (they're equipped with points you tack in place), then hang them from nails.

WALL ANCHORS

If you're hanging your picture on a hollow, wood-frame wall, you can simply drive your hanger or nail through the drywall or plaster. If your picture is especially heavy and you're hanging it on a hollow part of the wall, or if you're working on solid masonry walls, use screws in conjunction with wall anchors, which expand and grip inside the wall. A basic home improvement book will give you an illustrated chart of wall fasteners and tell you what sort of wall and weight each is best suited for. The folks at your local hardware store can also help guide you to the right hanger for the job. Anchors are available with hooks for hanging pictures. You can also screw D-rings into your frame, then hook the rings over standard anchored screws.

keeping it straight

The Placing Pictures steps on page 53 tell you how to gauge where to drive your hangers, nails, or screws into the wall, so your pictures hang exactly where you want them. If you're centering a series of pictures, make sure those placements line up along an imaginary center line, either horizontal or vertical, that bisects the hanging pieces. Use a metal tape measure and a level to check your positioning as you go. And to keep a picture from cocking to one side or the other, use the removable plastic adhesive sold for mounting unframed posters. Stick a small dot of the tacky substance, which looks something like modeling clay, between the backs of the picture's upper corners and the wall.

location

location location

The color of the walls and style of the furnishings shouldn't be your only considerations when you're choosing a location for a picture. Give the following factors some thought, too.

humidity

High humidity encourages mold—which can grow both on a picture's frame and inside, on the picture itself. Mold growth is least likely in a home with central heat and air. If you don't have those conveniences, inspect your home once a season to gauge the dampness of each room, and arrange your pictures accordingly. Fiber art, which readily absorbs liquid, should be displayed in the driest room. Save pictures sealed behind glass for more humid areas. In any home, felt bump-ons, which you mount on the back bottom edge of a picture, will prop your pieces off the wall and allow air to circulate. The high humidity of bathrooms and kitchens makes them poor locations for pictures that aren't sealed behind glass.

heat

Avoid placing valuable pieces over a fireplace during the months when you'll be using it. Heat can damage pictures, and real-wood fireplaces also emit soot particles. Instead, hang inexpensive seasonal decorations or inexpensive prints. Think twice before locating pictures near a heating vent; consider both the output of heat and the circulation of dust. Also, avoid placing pictures over stoves and ovens.

grease

It's not just the aroma of food that wafts through your home. Grease and other pollutants from cooking are carried on the air, too. In a short period of time, they can deposit a film on the surfaces of pictures. That means it's best not to display uncovered art in the kitchen or dining area. Instead, opt for pictures protected by glass—and be ceratin to clean the glass and frames regularly.

ultraviolet light

If you've read or listened to the news in the last decade, you know that mild, regular exposure to the sun's rays can be just as damaging to skin as a blistering dose of ultraviolet light. Pictures can suffer similar damage, so keep them out of direct sunlight. It speeds natural deterioration and can fade them after only a few weeks.

furniture

Don't position pictures where they'll bump into your furniture, be bumped by people trying to avoid bumping the furniture, or be bumped by people using your furniture. No-nos include placing pictures directly behind a piece of furniture that moves (such as a recliner) in a high-traffic area that already features a few furniture obstacles, or so low they'll come in contact with the head of anyone sitting on the couch.

children and pets

Never place pictures within reach of a child's arms or a dog's tail, so the adage goes. It would be great if life were that simple, but kids have legs and toys they swing with as much abandon as their arms, and dogs have chewing habits, sharp nails, and shedding fur in addition to tails. And did we mention that each can jump? If you have children or pets—or have some who regularly visit your home—your best bet is to display your most delicate or valuable pictures up high, and use common sense when placing the rest.

IF your household includes an artist in residence, you may need a hanging device that allows for the rapid and frequent turnover of shows. Shop the hardware section of a home improvement store for a metal strip of any kind. Some school supply stores also sell them, just for this purpose. Screw your strip into the wall beside the kitchen phone, between the bunk beds and the dresser, or just above the toy chest in the playroom. Add a set of magnets, and your gallery is ready to go. If you want to make it easy for your young virtuoso to also curate his or her own shows, be sure to hang the strip within reaching distance.

Most of the fuss about picture molding is that it lets you hang lots of different pieces without driving lots of nails into your walls. True enough. But just as important, it's such a graceful way to mount a display. If your picture frames are already equipped with screw eyes—which a professional framer will position just above the mid-point—and you want your pictures to hang flat against the wall rather than tilt forward from the top, move the screw eyes to the frame's top back corners. Simply remove them, use an awl to punch starting holes in the new spots, then screw them back in. Securely knot the ends of a strand of cord or ribbon to each screw eye, and use it to dangle your pictures (or even shadow boxes of souvenirs, as we have here) from molding hooks. You'll find the hooks—in various designs and in materials ranging from antique brass to polished nickel—at places that sell framing supplies and in many hardware stores.

IF YOU SOMEHOW NEGLECTED TO SET UP RESIDENCE IN A RESTORED VICTORIAN HOME already outfitted with miles of picture rails just below all the original crown molding, don't worry; you can still get the look. Any home improvement store will sell you ready-to-install molding. Most carry it in a number of styles, from something spare like we've used here to a type that's more ornate, curlicues and all. You can stain it or paint it to match your setting, then screw it in place exactly where you want it.

problem: Lots of meaningful little bits and pieces—postcards, snapshots, greeting cards, etc.—that you'd like to hang together rather than pack away in a keepsake box, never to be seen again.

solution: Depending on the size of your images, buy some of the accordion-style plastic photo holders meant for wallets and pocket-size photo books, or stop at a photography supply store and buy a few of the plastic sleeves made for organizing oversize transparencies. Use decorative tacks or pushpins to attach a series of the clear strips to a wall, and you have a flexible, functional display center.

AN inventive hanging apparatus can turn an ordinary picture display into a full-blown art installation. All you need is a horizontal bar that's not flush against the wall, so you can knot some rope or cord in place. Here, a piece of lumber attached with door handles provides the anchor for natural-colored rope. Metal pipes and multi-colored rock-climbing ropes would give the same setup a more playful feel. Polished metal towel bars and lengths of jute would make it more elegant. The less stretchy your rope or cord, the better; go ahead and test its stretch factor before hanging every-thing in place. When you're satisfied, knot one end of each rope to a screw eye on the back of the picture, as described on page 41. Secure the other to the hanging bar you've rigged up. Use a basic knot-tying guide to make sure the way you tie everything together is going to hold.

RETROFIT AN OLD MEDICINE CABINET OR KITCHEN CABINET WITH CLEAR GLASS SHELVES, and you flood it with openness and light—all the better to show off propped pictures and other objects.

OFF
the WALL

IF a setting already includes one or more of the following: floral wallpaper, satin, vintage photographs, antique furniture, or a pastel color scheme, why in the world would you simply hang your pictures directly on the wall? Some spaces are meant to be more ornamentally adorned. Suspending your pictures from thick widths of luxurious ribbon is the perfect way to add to the trimmings. Use taffeta, velvet, or some other closely woven, heavy ribbon, and pair it with small and/or light pictures. Staple the ribbon to the back of the frame with a staple gun, then reinforce its top edge, where it will hang, either by doubling the ribbon over or by using a grommet kit to insert a grommet. Give the display your signature by experimenting with both single and double lengths of ribbon and by trimming the ends with pinking shears or other specialty scissors. A decorative nail, such as a curtain tieback nail, makes a nice touch as a hanger.

at home with pictures

L ots of us got
our start in picture hanging by taping shots of celebrity heartthrobs to the inside of locker doors, tucking class photos into the edges of the bedroom mirror, and tacking magazine clippings on bulletin boards. If the carefree spirit of that casual, work-in-progress style still appeals to you years later, this page and the next show you ways to incorporate it into a more grown-up environment. Transform an indoor clothesline or two into contemporary looking display wires (above). Simply install them on your wall, then equip them with an interesting collection of binder clips, snap links, swivel hooks, and colored clothespins, all for holding up lightweight pictures and photos.

The nailed–together boards below create both an interesting backdrop and a big, rustic bulletin board, suspended with heavy rope from hooks in the ceiling. For the same idea in a different style, experiment with everything from fabric-covered insulation board and colored foam core to a piece of painted pegboard.

breaking the rules and getting away with it

Yes, pictures are supposed to hang from picture hangers. In flat formations against the wall. If they don't, as you can see, you risk all sorts of disorderly conduct—which just might lead somewhere interesting. This rambunctious combination of small shadow boxes and thick frames is layered two deep here and there, thanks to threaded rods and wing nuts acting as hangers. Measure the length of rod you need, adding together the thickness of the two frames you're layering and allowing for about ½ inch (1.3 cm) of rod in the wall. The home improvement store where you buy your rod can cut it for you, too. Install the rods with wall anchors (flip back to page 38), positioning two per picture, so you have just enough room to slide the picture into place between them. You'll hold the picture steady against the ones behind it by screwing wing nuts onto each rod. More a display device than a super-secure hanging technique, use this approach with lightweight pictures.

A **ctually meant** to hang
pajamas, jackets, and diaper
bags up and out of the way, this
menagerie of painted wooden
hooks makes a charming set of
display hangers for pictures suspended from ribbon. The easy
idea lends itself to all sorts of
styles. Use shiny metal kitchen
hooks to hang black-and-white
photos from thin cable or chain
links. Try hammered-tin hooks
featuring fish and rope or jute to
show off the wood-framed pictures of your trip to the Adiron-
dacks. Or mount small glass vintage knobs in the bathroom and
use them to suspend tiny cameos
from strips of fabric or lace. Flip
back to page 45 for instructions
on attaching ribbon, cord, or
another hanger to a picture.

at home with pictures

OFF
the WALL

GALLERY LEDGES COME IN DIFFERENT LENGTHS AND DEPTHS, lots of styles, and with and without lips on the front edge to prevent objects from slipping off. They make it easy to install a horizontal surface anywhere you need one, then casually lap leaning pictures in front of one another.

This pretty little variation

on the classic technique of suspending pictures from ribbon or cord incorporates the picture's screw-eye hangers right into the design. Instead of hiding them on the back of the frame's top corners, screw them into the top edge. Use one ribbon to make the triangle-shaped hanger. Tie a sturdy bow at the top of the triangle, then stitch through the knot several times to secure it. Tie the end of the central ribbon around the center of the bow. Again, make a sturdy knot, and stitch through it several times. Trim the ends of the ribbons for a crisp look. If you prefer fanciful and flowing, leave them long.

arranging

Picture arranging is one of those subjects that attracts an overabundance of rules. Forget them all for a minute, and think mood. What you're really doing when you decide how you want to group together a few pictures is helping to establish a room's tone or attitude—calm or active, cozy or luxurious, orderly or spontaneous, and so on. Think first about the mood you want to set, then use the following techniques and tips as guidelines to achieve it.

placing pictures

Maybe you want regimented rows, a single graphic strip, two asymmetrical clusters, or a mass arrangement that fills an entire wall. Or, more likely, maybe you don't yet know exactly *what* you want. Playing around with placement right on your walls is the best way to decide what works best where. Here's a clever way to do it that doesn't leave your walls full of experimental holes.

1 Trace all the pictures you think you want to work with onto pieces of paper (paper bags work well), and cut out the shapes.

2 If the backs of the framed pictures are equipped with hanging wire, pull the wire taut on each, and measure from the top of the wire's arc to the top of the frame. On the matching paper template, measure down from the top edge the distance of your measurement, and mark where the picture–hanging nail or hook will meet the wire. If the backs of your pictures feature saw-toothed hangers rather than wire, measure how far down they are from the top edge of each picture, and transfer those marks to the corresponding templates.

3 Use a low-tack tape (both drafting tape and painter's tape work well) to hang the templates on the wall (marked sides facing out), then reconfigure them as much as you like, until you're happy with where each is hanging.

4 Hammer your nails (and picture hooks, if you're using them) through the marks on the templates and right into the wall; then rip the paper off and hang your pictures.

classic groupings

Nearly any arrangement is going to be a variation on one of the following standard themes. If you have a stack of pictures and a blank wall to fill but no idea where to start, experiment with fitting your pictures into a few of these forms.

TOPS OR BOTTOMS IN ALIGNMENT

Draw together a group of various-size pictures by aligning all their tops or all their bottoms along an imaginary horizontal line.

COMBINATION ALIGNMENT

Divide a larger group of various-size pictures into two or more rows, and align the tops of the top-row pictures and the bottoms of the bottom-row pictures on imaginary hori-zontal lines; then align the sides as well.

MOSAIC

Anything goes, with a bit of method to the madness. Give your mosaic display some balance by aligning the bottoms of some frames with the tops of others and/or by centering some pictures over others. You can also soften a rigid-looking arrangement by adding in a few rounded or octagonal frames.

FOUR CORNERS

Define your space, and place your four largest pictures at the corners. Use your smaller pictures to fill in the middle.

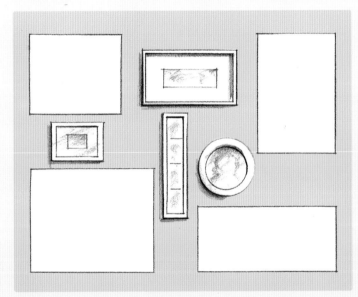

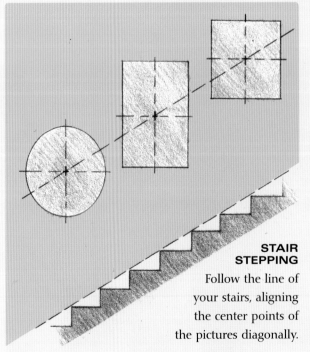

GALLERY STYLE

Hang identical-size pictures in a long, neat row, either horizontal or vertical. You may want to use a string secured with pushpins to establish a hanging guide.

STAIR STEPPING

Follow the line of your stairs, aligning the center points of the pictures diagonally.

space relations

REGARDLESS of the colors and styles you have to work with and the choices you make in terms of mats and frames, decorating your home with pictures is essentially about arranging objects in a space. Here are some of the most common situations you're likely to run up against while piecing together the puzzle.

TIGHT FITS

Start with a room's architectural elements—windows, door frames, chimneys, built-in shelves—then add all the furniture and accessories, and you may be left with just a few snug spots for pictures. Fortunately, those spots can also offer the most interesting places for emphasizing photos, paintings, and other art. Work with single pieces whose shapes fit the spaces, as we have here, or group several small ones.

space relations

HAPPY SURPRISES

It's good to hang pictures where the eye expects
to see them; we sense something is missing if the
wall above the couch or the fireplace is empty.
But it can be even better to hang pictures in less
predictable places—under an eave, on a small
cupboard door, inside the guest closet, even on
the small patch of wall beneath a window.

WIDE-OPEN WALLS

Other times, you may have too much bare wall
space to fill, especially in areas such as long hall–
ways, where you don't have the help of lots of fur–
niture. A good solution is to cut the area in half
with a chair rail, a wallpaper border, or a clever
paint job like the one here. Instantly, you have two
smaller visual spaces. This row of standard-size
pictures is perfectly in proportion in the top space.

space tips

■ You can visually open up a small room by hanging a landscape featuring a faraway vista. It adds a "window" to the outdoors.

■ Strong horizontal lines in a picture tend to be calming and can make narrow rooms appear wider.

■ Strong vertical lines in a picture tend to make low-ceilinged rooms appear taller.

QUIRKS

Every home has a few. Maybe it's a place where the wall juts out, over, and back in again to conceal a chimney pipe. Or perhaps it's a window-size cutout, like this one, opening one room to another. Whatever your particular structural twists, have some fun with them. Here, the picture beside the cutout, which mimics it almost perfectly, turns the opening into a second work of art.

how many, how high & how far apart

■ Our eyes respond positively to logical groupings, so start by clustering your pictures in pairs
or threes. Odd-numbered groups are generally more
dynamic, because they imply a focal point with an
even number of others surrounding the hub. Even
groupings often have a more calming, ordered effect.
If you want to quickly transform an even-numbered
grouping into odd, toss in a wild-card element—a
mirror, a carving, a hanging tile.

■ Unless you intend for an entire room to revolve
around a dramatic piece of art, it's easiest to fig-
ure out picture-hanging height, width, and general
placement if you position all your furniture first.
Typically, you don't want a group of pictures to be
wider than the furniture piece below them. If they're
narrower, they should be at least half the length of the
furniture. The bottom of the group of pictures should
be close enough to the table, couch, or whatever else
they're above to relate to it, but still have some breathing room—about 8 to 10 inches (20.3 to 30.5 cm).

■ One of the most common picture-placing mis-
takes is hanging pieces too high. Unless you're
trying to achieve an austere look, you want your pictures at eye level, which expert picture hangers say is
usually 3 or 4 inches (7.6 or 10.2 cm) lower than where
you think it is. When you're figuring eye level, also
think about the space's primary function. In a dining
room or living room, where people are seated most
of the time, set eye level at about 5 or 6 inches
(12.7 or 15.2 cm) above the backs of couches or chairs.
In a hallway, on the other hand, you probably want
your pictures at or just above eye level.

■ In most situations, you want several inches of
space around each picture in a group. If they're
too close, they lose their individuality. Too far apart,
they have no unity.

weighty matters

Hang lighter pieces over heavier ones, and
the result is harmonious balance. Reverse
the arrangement, and you invite viewers to
move in and inspect the bottom piece. When
you're playing with weight distribution, keep
in mind that heaviness is determined not just
by size, but also by the color and material
of your pictures. A small, dark painting in
a strong mahogany frame might well feel
heavier than a larger one featuring airy
pastels and no frame at all.

picture care

Regular maintenance will keep all your framed pieces pretty as a picture.

a quick touch-up

For frequent cleaning, just focus on your picture's frame and the glass.

THE FRAME

A moderately stiff brush works best for cleaning sturdy frames with relief or embedded designs, or with secure surface decoration. Brush away from the picture inside. You'll be amazed to see how much dust flies from between the nooks and crannies. A stiff brush is also ideal for brushing lint and dirt from cloth-backed picture frames and from sturdy cloth frames, such as velvet. Apply only gentle pressure and brush in only one direction—again, away from the picture. You can also use a lint brush or a piece of adhesive to remove small fuzz and debris. For solid frames or those with delicate finishes, dust the front and back and on all sides with a dry, soft, lint-free cloth.

THE GLASS

Dust the glass with a duster or a dry, soft, lint-free cloth. Then, spray a small amount of glass cleaner onto another cloth. (Never spray cleaner directly on the glass. It will drip between the glass and frame and onto the picture inside.) Wipe the glass in smooth, gentle strokes, and avoid leaving streaks or dirt trails on the glass. If you find that dust has worked its way into the corners or along the edge where the glass and frame meet, dislodge it with a dry toothbrush.

detailing

Once a year or so, you may want to clean your framed pieces more thoroughly. They likely fall into one of two categories: pieces that are covered with glass and pieces that aren't.

PICTURES BEHIND GLASS

For pictures behind glass that weren't professionally matted and framed, it's best to remove the frame to clean them. Professionally framed pictures shouldn't collect dust or dirt behind the glass, so the Quick Touch-Up, left, should do.

After removing the picture, dust it lightly with a dry, soft, lint-free cloth; then set it aside, so it doesn't come in contact with the glass cleaner. Use the tips above for cleaning the glass and frame, being careful of the glass's sharp edges.

UNCOVERED PICTURES

Dust pictures that aren't covered with glass (most often oil paintings) with a lint-free silk cloth or a very soft brush, with one exception. Do NOT brush or dust a pastel or charcoal drawing. You'll wipe the artwork away. If you notice a spot of dirt, blot it gently with a slightly damp rag. If the spot doesn't come off, consult a professional framer about further cleaning. Follow the tips at the left for cleaning the frame. Be extra careful to brush or dust away from the picture; one wild swing of the brush, and you could cause permanent damage.

If any picture is of great value—either monetary or sentimental—consult a professional framer about cleaning it. It's costly, if not impossible, to repair damage.

W hen some other element provides the order in a group of pictures, you're free to play around with abstract collage when it comes to hanging configurations. Here, it's mostly unifying colors that provide the organization. Compatible shapes or subject matter can work, too. The connecting element makes the display spirited rather than chaotic, by taking viewers by the hand and leading them through the sequence.

Stacking these same–size frames

and filling them with mats with multiple openings is a cost-effective way to create a commanding visual presence. In addition to being less expensive than a single frame large enough to fill the entire space, the stacked sequence creates a rhythmic grid that gives a group of various-size photos a graphic framework. It also repeats the pattern of the wooden panes on the nearby windows.

breaking
the
rules
and getting away with it

T his **sequence** of stacked frames, similar to the one on the preceding page, defies the picture-hanging precept that bigger, heavier pieces belong on the bottom of a vertical group. Balanced here by lamps at each side, the funnel-shaped configuration provides a pleasing sense of movement.

IF you have
a set of pictures you want to stand out, sometimes the hanging style that's best is one that eliminates all other distraction. These two centered, precisely aligned rows of heavy-handed frames make sure the push and pull of the photographs themselves create the rhythm in an otherwise stable setting. The ordered, gallery-style arrangement also makes it easy for subtle outside elements—from shadows to streams of sunlight—to help bring the display to life.

Create a central axis by stacking these two photos on top of each other, and they'd feel right at home. They'd also look perfectly paired side by side on a horizontal line. But if you consider the subject matter—these are kids in motion, after all, not heirloom portraits of great-grandparents—the slightly off-kilter arrangement gives the display a charming boost. The stained-glass pieces in the upper windows provide symmetrical bookends, just so the off-center style doesn't get too out of hand.

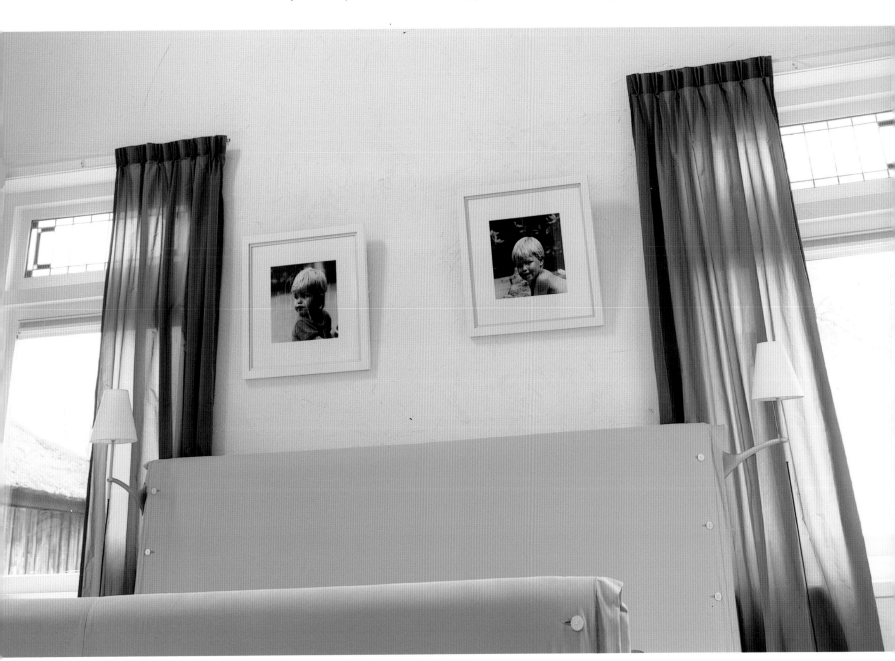

IF it hasn't happened already,

at some point in your picture-arranging career you'll probably decide that nice, solid blocks and contained little rows are too quiet and settled for a certain group of pictures, a certain setting, or your current frame of mind. Here's a reminder that the energy of points, angles, and even the interaction between two walls might better suit some situations.

OFF the WALL

PROVIDE THE DIMENSIONS, AND A CUSTOM FRAMER CAN CUT LARGE SECTIONS OF MAT to fit the glass doors of a hutch, wardrobe, or even a section of your kitchen cabinets. Secure them in place with push points, also known as glazier points—the same little gadgets used to hold the back of a mirror or picture in place.

at home with pictures

These
color-block
canvases lend themselves especially well to the hanging style known as *combination alignment*, a method of evening up the top, bottom, and outside edges of a large group of various-size pictures. Whatever sorts of images you're working with, the fun comes in the geometric puzzle of piecing together the multiple edges within the tidy block.

problem solving

problem: A wide, empty wall (low-placed furniture and accessories create the challenge here), and only a few small compositions to fill it with.

solution: Carve out a smaller space within the enormity. This pale green backing obligingly defines a wall within a wall, helping the cluster of smaller works claim their position. A sheet of interior-grade plywood, a piece of neatly trimmed sheetrock, even an interesting piece of fabric, are all options for creating this sort of space-filling link, giving the same last name to a disparate family of rectangular shapes. The color of the backing piece is critical here, too, helping the picture group balance out the lush, green plant.

at home with pictures

Classic hanging styles can be

adapted to suit more than one personality type. The free spirit who lives with the artsy assemblage on this page is a salon-style extremist who maintains that kitsch and baroque blend just fine, stops and starts when filling a space are permissible, and a wall of pictures is meant to be revelled in. Her more ordered counterpart, who resides in the room on the next page, also believes that life is full, and pictures on a wall are a wonderful way to celebrate it. But she admits to favoring a bit of alignment here and there, patterns of repeated shapes, and an anchoring central piece.

The spirit of salon–style arrangements is this: even though you want to cram a lot onto a small wall, there's no reason it can't look good. Perfected by the more-is-more Victorians, salon-style configurations look as if they were poured onto the wall, the bottom layer filling up first and the others piling on top, until the entire arrangement forms its own, autonomous shape. Leaving every last minimalist sensibility behind, salon style happily embraces pictures and frames of widely different styles, weights, colors, and designs.

M aybe you have a setting—or just a personal style—that finds an entire group of even casually hung pictures too formal. Here's permission to take carefree to the extreme. This family of photos looks as if it's yawning, stretching, and slowly moving itself up and into position. For now, it's happy to let some members hang as wall art while others lag behind, propping themselves up as display objects on a shelf. The matching frames help the cluster of rectangles assume a pose that's artful as opposed to sloppy, while the natural-wood frame in the next room links the two spaces, suggesting that there is, after all, a plan, relaxed though it may be.

More often than not, it's all of a room's other elements—the bed, the bookcase, the chairs, the desk—that claim their wall space first. Pictures are often the last to squeeze their way in. The more actively they interact with all that prearranged furniture and the more neatly they fit the leftover space, the more likely they are to look as if they belong. This high horizontal strip of photos perfectly punctuates the bed's plain, bare headboard. Another picture from the same sequence hangs off on its own, distributing the photographic theme into the rest of the room.

The eye craves
the order of familiar shapes. But it also delights in some playful tweaking of the patterns

it's come to expect. The simple pairing of a long, horizontal piece with two smaller pictures to form
a classic block gives the display on the left a touch of added interest. The not-quite-perfect diamond-
shape cluster below gently pulls from side to side, keeping it from settling into the static state a
more aligned arrangement might. The interplay of frame styles and color also helps the pictures
seem as if they're prepared to skip around their four positions, rather than sit completely still.

INSTALL A ROW OF CLOSELY PLACED COAT HOOKS or shelf brackets to create an inventive propping ledge anywhere you need one. Rest larger pictures right on the hooks or brackets themselves. For smaller pictures and other objects, settle a narrow piece of painted plywood over the hooks or brackets, and use it as a shelf.

A block-style arrangement always brings order to a group of pictures, but you've still got a choice about whether you want that order to feel reassuringly settled or offer some visual activity. These four simple line drawings on the right, all in weighty wooden frames, sit solidly in place. Their classic, symmetrical arrangement and tight spacing give them a fixed presence and reinforce that they're functioning as a single unit. Though the four photos below also form a unified block, their staggered pattern—vertical, horizontal, vertical, horizontal—lets them spin ever so slightly around a central hub. The variety of photo size and matting style also adds some gentle movement as the eye rotates from one identical frame to another.

color schemes

Ask everyone from cultural anthropologists to child psychologists: color affects how we think and feel. Not far behind these experts are paint manufacturers and interior decorators, reminding us that color has perhaps the most significant impact of any single element on how our living spaces look. One color can make a formal room more cozy. Another can transform a dark corner into a bright and airy one. One side of the color wheel will tend to make a space seem cool and calm. The other will enliven it and heat it up. In other words, how you use color has a great deal to do with the mood of any room.

Pictures play a key role in all kinds of color schemes. They can help highlight accent colors that might otherwise fade away, provide a single burst of color in a neutral space, unify touches of color throughout a room, or saturate a space by repeating its dominant color theme.

MAKE SURE YOUR PICTURES INTERACT WITH THEIR SETTING TO CREATE THE COLOR PATTERNS YOU WANT BY KEEPING THESE BASIC GUIDELINES IN MIND:

walls. If you're living in a perfect world, go ahead and repaint all your walls to harmonize perfectly with your pictures. If you dwell more frequently in the real world, then simply give some thought to the color tones you want to emphasize when you put your pictures in contact with walls, and make small adjustments along the way. In some cases, the adjustment might be as easy as moving a picture from an off-white wall in the dining room to a sunny yellow wall in the kitchen. Other times, you may decide it's worth the effort to alter the shade of a couple of walls so they better complement or contrast with a colorful collection of pictures.

accessories. Whether you want to bring out the strong blues in a painting or echo the black–and–white graphics in a framed poster, one of the easiest ways to do it is with accessories—from rugs and curtains to lamp shades and throw pillows. Think about the color combinations these sorts of pieces have already established in a room before you choose which pictures to hang among them. At the same time, be open to moving objects around. If packing away the green vase and putting a royal purple one in its place helps highlight a picture's dominant shades, go forth and rearrange.

location. Specifically, light. Consider how much sun a room gets and at what time of day. Morning light, for example, will make colors appear cooler than late-after-noon light. A north-facing room will likely feel colder and darker in terms of color tone. Think, too, about whether you'll spend most of your time in the room during daylight hours or at night, when artificial lights will affect its colors and atmosphere.

mats & frames. How you set off your pictures can have a lot to do with the color qualities they communicate. A rich, gilded frame, for example, will emphasize a piece's warm tones. Brushed metal or aluminum might make it look cooler or more stark—or bring out its pinks, blues, and grays. A dark mat will tend to intensify a picture's colors. The thinner and more subtle the mat, the more the picture's colors will interact with their surroundings.

the right light

A Pink Floyd poster without a black light, the Radio City Rockettes without a spotlight, a romantic dinner under fluorescents—all examples of lighting that's not quite right. To achieve the mood, effect, or reaction you want, you need the right lighting. And so do your pictures.

SUNLIGHT destroys, art causing premature fading and other damage. It's also unreliable and inflexible (ever try telling the sun when to position itself just so?). You're better off relying on a well-planned installation of artificial light with the right type and wattage of bulbs. Here are four general lighting methods to choose from, based on your pictures, their location, and your budget.

PICTURE LIGHTS service individual pictures. They're available at home stores and attach easily to frames or to the wall above, below, or alongside a picture. Best of all, they come in clever styles that can complement what they're illuminating. For instance, several companies make lens-style picture lights. What better choice for spotlighting black-and-white photos? You can also turn mini-lights into picture lights by stringing them around a frame. There are three options for powering picture lights: plug in the cord at the nearest outlet; have an electrician place an outlet behind the picture; or have an electrician wire the device into your electrical system in the wall. (The latter is really a plan-ahead option only; it's best taken care of during the construction of your home.)

PORTABLE FLOOR LIGHTS are low-sitting canisters that cast light up. You can position them on any flat surface to create a dramatic spotlight for what's hanging above them.

TRACK LIGHTS can illuminate multiple pictures and provide room lighting at the same time. They're also an inexpensive, flexible way to light your pictures. Mounted on the ceiling, track lights can be installed anywhere on the track, and angled to strike pictures where they hang or to bathe a wall in light, giving nearby pictures a subtle glow. If you decide to relocate a picture within the room, adjusting the lighting is a simple matter of re-angling a light bulb.

RECESSED LIGHTS are unobtrusive and can provide individual picture lighting. Unfortunately, they can also be expensive to install, since they're placed in a ceiling, wall, or piece of furniture. Some types of recessed lights feature bulbs that can be angled into various positions, much like track lights.

bulb by bulb

INCANDESCENT

They're not as long-lasting or energy-efficient as other bulbs, but if you want a warm, unobtrusive glow that brings out a picture's richness and depth, incandescents are the way to go.

HALOGEN

Pay a little more, and you get a bulb that lasts thousands of hours. Their brilliant light can give your pictures intense illumination. The downside is that they burn extremely hot. Don't place halogens close to your pictures, and connect them to a dimmer switch, if possible.

COMPACT FLUORESCENT

These bulbs, adapted from office tubes, have a lot going for them. They last 10 times longer than incandescents, and use one-third the electricity to produce the same level of light. Straight-tube fluorescents can saturate an area with concentrated light and work especially well in recessed fixtures.

SPECIALTY

From frosted to colored to full-spectrum bulbs that mimic sunlight, there are lots of specialty options on the market. If you're using tinted or colored bulbs, keep these guidelines in mind: cool-colored bulbs enhance blues and grays; warm-colored bulbs amplify yellow, red, and most shades of wood; frosted bulbs diffuse light.

at home with pictures

AS spectacular as the spiral staircase, as grand as the vaulted ceilings, there's no question as to where your eye will go first when you walk into this entry space. It latches onto the two brilliant red paintings. Another sliver of the same color peeks out from the next room. The neat visual path demonstrates how, by eliminating virtually all color, then adding back a few bold splashes, you can choreograph where people look and even how traffic patterns flow.

The warm wood grains of the floor and table and the leafy green of the chairs concentrate most of this room's color in its lower half. By borrowing from those big pools and pulling a bit of the color into the white void above, this painting completes the tranquil, unified setting. If your goal was to make the room spring to life, you might substitute a picture featuring intense reds, yellows, or blues. The room's greens and browns then would act as an underpinning for the focal-point painting above.

Remove the
color contrasts of warm and cold, pure and dull, and
variations in hue, and you're left with a study of light and dark. This
elegant display of white, black, and gray, accented only by brushed silver,
emphasizes the intricate lines of the images—allowing them to sing.

breaking
the and
rules getting away
with it

T ypically,
we think of
pictures and their mats
as the places for bringing out color in a display. But here's a display that
uses frames and the wall, instead, to electrify an area. Craft stores sell
inexpensive unfinished frames, so you can paint them exactly the shade you
want—or paint a series in a progressive color sequence, as we have here.
Hang the frames without their backing or glass, then use pushpins to tack
small pictures inside, letting the wall provide a mat-like border in between.

T hink of it as an art installation

curated by theme. Think of its title as *Mom & Apple Pie.* Most of all, think of it as sheer fun. Anytime you use a mix of pure primary and secondary colors, the message is one of lively, happy activity—perfect for framing this tribute to childhood and home for a playroom or bedroom wall.

If you'd like to display the same subject matter but in a more elegant way, try frames with a more subdued color scheme, and you instantly elevate the look. In the setting on the left, the noticeable color contrast is provided by the walls and flowers. The quiet interplay of black and gray frames simply keeps the display from seeming static.

OFF
the WALL

THE HOLIDAYS ARE FULL OF TABLETOP OPTIONS for hanging ornaments without actually dragging needle-shedding evergreens inside, everything from vintage wire trees and handcrafted wooden variations with swinging arms to customized metal spirals like this one. Personalize yours completely by using wide lengths of ribbon to display cameo pictures along with your other decorations.

at home with pictures

Take the intensity out of the color of the walls, and these oversize photos of flowers and green foliage would feel serene rather than brilliantly alive. Though their presence would still be commanding against a neutral cream or gray backdrop, the softer color would tone down their impact, allowing them to enfold a viewer into their space. Instead, the tension created here by wall and picture colors that aren't quite complementary causes the setting to vibrate with energy.

problem
solving

problem: A busy room that lacks focus.

solution: Hang a big, colorful centerpiece; then quiet down everything around it. Think of it this way. If you fill a room with 25 people all talking at the top of their lungs, you won't be able to make out a thing. But if a couple of people are carrying on a spirited dialogue, there's more of a chance for you to engage. Let a single, vivid image like this one do the talking, and make sure the rest of the room's colors and accessories just chime in every now and then. Here, that's accomplished with small splashes of the picture's prominent colors in other objects throughout the room and with a succession of thin, vertical shapes that echo the picture's color bars.

These two
nearly identical, neutral rooms demonstrate the difference the color of a picture can make. In the room on the left, the strong fuschias and pinks of the painting provide virtually the only saturated color in the room. They stimulate the space, causing the room's more understated colors—the sage green and canvas, the brushed metal and black—to appear to bump up a notch now that they have something to react to. The minimalist painting in the room below, on the other hand, simply reinforces the space's much more muted play of white on white. The most contrast a viewer can hope for here is the reserved difference between a yellow tint and a bluish cast, depending on the angle of the light.

I magine a color wheel—or better yet, a box of crayons. All the reds, oranges, and yellows are neatly slotted on one side. The blues, purples, and greens fill the other. The comforting appeal of this painting in this room is that it mimics that familiar balance. The warm end of the color spectrum is expressed in the painting's charming, brush-stroked squares. The colors from the cooler end then group themselves in small vignettes—the lamps, the vases, the folded blanket—that are dotted throughout the room.

IN this cool, almost colorless room, the slightest note of any vivid shade would pop and sing. Instead, the formal cluster of four rhythmic, graphic, black-and-white images keeps the eye focused on pattern, line, and contrasts in light and dark. In a more traditional setting, the wall and floor colors would likely be reversed. Here, the steely blue-gray walls give the pictures' wide white mats added punch, making the pictures themselves even more of a focal point.

THE OFFICIAL NAME FOR GLASS-PANELED DISPLAY CASES LIKE THIS ONE IS *VITRINE*. But whatever you call them, small, museum-style cabinets can elevate the pictures and other mementos inside to the level of prized presentation pieces. Shops and mail-order companies that specialize in picture frames sell them.

OFF
the WALL

This painting's big splash of active color all but pulls up a seat and enters into the conversation at the table—then invites everything, from the rambunctious tablecloth and purple bench to the candles, dishes, and painted chairs, to dance. Still, white is the most important color in any display this cheerfully dense. The stark walls provide it here. They give all the rest some space to breathe, so the effect is energizing as opposed to smothering.

themes

P eople who hang pictures for a living in galleries and museums are often faced with an array of diverse pieces—different sizes, different colors, different styles, different frames—and their challenge is to decide how to unite them. Sound familiar? When you're dealing with the same problem at home, use the same approach they often do: group your pictures by theme.

A theme is any motif that makes sense to you—all land-scapes, all photographs of fruit, all works by the same artist, all watercolors in blue. Choosing a common thread to empha-size makes it easier to make decisions about which pictures you want to include in a particular display and which are better to save for another. It can also guide you in starting with just a piece or two and building a collection—*You know, I really love the red poppies in that painting. I'm going to look for a few more pictures with red flowers to hang with it.* Most of all, it's one of the best ways to create a display that has presence, range, synchronicity, and a distinctive personality.

tips for grouping pictures by theme

■ Limit the number of pictures you include. You'll be able to more effectively reinforce their similarities, and their differences will be less distracting.

■ A unified theme doesn't always produce a unified look. In addition to combining pictures by subject matter, try to include pieces that have some similarities in terms of texture, color, shape, or size, or that work together to create a certain level of intensity or a sense of balance.

■ Reinforce the fact that the pictures belong together by putting them in close proximity. Place them too far apart, and there's a chance the connections they have will lose their impact. Instead, you want their similarities to appear to touch, even overlap.

■ Use repetition. Most often, you'll be featuring repetition of subject matter (five photographs of your grandparents, for example, or half a dozen drawings of houses). But think about repeating other elements as well. Maybe all the photographs are in oval frames, or all the drawings are thin line drawings. At the same time, try to avoid the monotony of complete duplication. It's better if the repeated shapes, patterns, or other elements can echo each other without being identical.

■ There are plenty of ways to create harmonious theme displays, even if your pictures share none of the same subject matter. Consider grouping pictures by medium (all woodblock prints or all paper collages), by historical period, by general style (all whimsical or all bold and contemporary), or even by proportion (all tiny images in the middle of spacious backgrounds), or rhythm (all featuring subjects in groups of three).

Some theme displays naturally transform themselves into tributes—to a person, a place, or a particular passion. Oftentimes, you want those tributes to be more inviting than dynamic, more a quiet narrative than a single vision that shouts its message from across the room. This ordered collection of vineyard shots, wine labels, and related pieces of paraphernalia encourages viewers to first spend time viewing hanging images, then move on to standing pictures, and, finally, all the way down to the small framed shots in the display case below.

OFF the WALL

THE SIMPLEST AND MOST OBVIOUS WAY TO GET AROUND DIGGING OUT THE HAMMER and putting holes in your walls is to just prop your pictures—along a chair rail, a shelf, a piece of molding, or the back edge of a counter, table, or other piece of furniture. Feel free to layer, overlap, and change the tableau every five minutes, if you like. The effect is gallery-style work in progress.

Most of us aren't fretting about finding just the right spot to hang the Picassos or the Monets. We're wondering what to do with that theme group of all theme groups: family photos. We're talking class pictures, kids in Halloween costumes, Grandma and Grandpa on their cruise, all the cousins in the pool. Not to mention the boxes of decades-old black-and-white photos you just moved out of your great-aunt's attic. When it starts to hit you that refrigerator magnets alone aren't going to do it anymore, consider some of these ideas.

Let portraits and photographs play off each other to enrich a spread-out display. A classic way to arrange standing photos on flat surfaces is to form them loosely into a triangle, with the taller, larger pictures in the back (in this case, at the triangle's tip).

Mats with multiple openings are the perfect way to contain a cluster of related family photos. Use the series of openings to lead the viewer through a visual story of a single family member's life or several generations of one family, or to showcase a bunch of family branches at once.

themes within the theme

If ever there were a picture category deserving of some strategic subdividing, its the stack (dare we say boxes?) of family photos. Here are some ways to break yours into smaller display groups.

BY GENERATION. Maybe you want to focus on various aspects of a single generation (pictures of celebrations, individuals, people at work and traveling), or create a linear display of single shots leading from one generation to another.

BY FAMILY BRANCH. Use multiple-opening mats to mount a photographic family tree.

CHRONOLOGICALLY. Set out a photographic tour of an individual's life or of a family's growth and changes over time.

BY EVENT. Cluster all the wedding photos, all the reunion photos, all the graduation photos, all the birthday photos, and so on.

BY ROOM. Hang holiday dinner shots in the kitchen, baby's first bath photos in the bathroom, shots of your grandparents in front of their store in your study, etc.

BY SEASON. Set aside an accessible space (maybe a shelf or a hall table) for a changing exhibit of shots of kids with Easter baskets, summer picnic pictures, and photos of everyone gathered around the turkey and cranberry sauce.

Break up larger groups to create small vignettes. These three photos connect not only as family pieces, but because of their age, their sepia tones, their female subjects, and the silver coloring in all three frames.

at home with pictures

This full-blown tribute to Americana is a brilliant example of what themed groupings do best: provide the order of unity and the vitality of variety all at once. Grounded in the fact that the flag is our motif, we're game for the wide range of colors, styles, and shapes, from bleached blues to rich reds, formal to folk art, and from traditional rectangles to the abstract flag forming a valance over the window.

Rather than hit you over the head, this

thematic display quietly unfolds. The
subjects of the sepia-tone images—
tree leaves and a flower—are related,
but the connection is more that of
cousins than of close siblings. Their
shared shapes are subtly reinforced by
the flowers and leafy trees in the wallpaper background, then reiterated
vividly with a vase of fresh flowers on
a pedestal that serves as the pictures'
centering point. Hanging the three
pieces slightly out of symmetry with
each other keeps the serene subject
matter from becoming static.

Maybe they're the faces of obscure poets you admire. Maybe they're all your favorite teachers from college. Or maybe they're just high-concept magazine ads for black turtlenecks. In other words, if these people all have a connection point, wonderful; your theme has another layer. But if they don't, the display is still a striking one with a clear and effective theme: head shots. You could mount a sleek, black-and-white matted row of similarly focused photos of anything from babies' feet to martini glasses.

breaking the rules

and getting away with it

Squelch the snippy voice in your head that keeps nattering on about how your pictures need to perfectly match the style of your furnishings. The only element these fanciful paintings of furniture pieces have in common with the real thing below is their subject matter, period. The interplay of whimsical and serious styles—animated images hanging from broad, colorful ribbons above formal furniture in a pristine room—is what makes the entire setting sparkle.

There are
lots of advantages to immersing yourself in a place—
its geography, architecture, natural history, and people. It's also
a satisfying way to organize a thematic display. You can include
everything from building blueprints and aerial photographs to
paintings by local artists and photos of the region's folk heros.

problem: You want to create a display to commemorate an important trip, but you have a dozen envelopes of photos and a suitcase full of souvenirs to work with.

solution: First, force yourself to edit. Yes, every picture has a story to tell, and each piece has meaning behind it. Nevertheless, find the fun in the challenge of picking out just a few—pictures and objects that not only give an overall sense of your journey, but also form some interesting connections in terms of color and shape. Second, hang them in a way that sets them off as a unified group. Here, shadow boxes all the same style and a suspension system of thin cables and chrome hooks do the job. Shops and mail-order companies that specialize in photo display products sell the systems. You can achieve the same unifying effect any number of ways, from hanging all your pieces from the same-color cord to positioning them all on a wall painted a different color from the rest of the room.

The bond among the pictures in this group? They're all large-scale shots of the ordinary. The entire display, situated in the most utilitarian room of the house, is an invitation to take a closer look at common objects and scenes. Consider other ways to mingle proportion, perspective, and motif—maybe a group of tiny photographs of houses, each surrounded by a huge mat, or pictures of shoes in one long row, and pictures of hats in another row below them.

AN EMPTY PICTURE FRAME CAN CREATE A HANDY LITTLE NOOK
between its back edge and the wall where it's attached. Tack it in
place at the bottom as well as the top, then tuck picture postcards,
hand-drawn doodles, and other informal images into the nook, and
let them strike an appropriately nonchalant pose.

OFF the WALL

combinations

Few of us live compartmentalized lives.

Instead, one activity bleeds over into another; priorities blend; lines blur; and, if we're lucky, it all somehow flows together. It makes sense that we'd often want the displays that represent those multifaceted lives to blend and flow, too. Instead of pictures over here and mementos, souvenirs, and other decorative objects over there, lots of times it looks more natural—not to mention more interesting and engaging—to mingle things together in creative combinations.

why combine

WHETHER YOU'RE HANGING PAINTINGS NEXT TO PIECES OF HANDMADE POTTERY or propping photographs and wooden flutes along a picture rail, here are some of the top reasons to combine pictures and other pieces.

■ **To add dimension.** Sometimes, in some settings, a group of nothing but flat pictures can look a little...flat. Mix in other objects to introduce additional shapes, textures, colors, or weights or to break up a bland pattern.

■ **To tell a story.** A framed photograph taken during your trip to Peru is nice. But hang that photograph alongside the colorful, hand-dyed bag you bought at one of the local markets and a map of your hike through the Andes, and you've created a richer narrative that draw viewers in.

■ **To set a mood.** Put a pitcher full of raucous wildflowers next to an oil painting of a landscape, and you soften it up and make it more accessible. Pair the same painting with a crystal vase holding a symmetrical arrangement of roses, and it's suddenly more formal.

■ **To heighten or soften colors.** Want the red sled and hat in the photo of your kids playing in the snow to pop? Hang a collage of red mittens beside it. Combine wooden carvings with a brightly painted mask, and they'll help connect it with the wooden table and chairs in the room.

■ **To create a context.** Try pairing pictures with objects that offer a framework, and the whole display becomes more meaningful—a stack of your grandfather's old books beneath his portrait, maybe, or a pile of stones beside a photo of the New foundland coast where you collected them.

■ **To elevate the ordinary.** You can use pictures to transform utilitarian objects into still-life vignettes, whether you hang small prints of herbs above your spice rack or photos of swimming pools beside your basket of bath towels.

M any times, when you combine pictures and other objects, you're also combining shapes. If that's the case, it can help the overall composition if you choose one shape and make it dominant. Here, for example, we see circles and ovals in both objects and in the decorative design of the hanging hardware. We also see triangles, formed by the hanging chains. Still, rectangles dominate the scene. Give viewers a hint at hierarchy in a mixed group like this one, and additional shapes will enrich rather than jumble a display.

breaking the rules and getting away with it

Conventional wisdom goes like this. If you want to display a group of wildly disparate pictures and objects and achieve balance as opposed to utter chaos, keep your number of items to a minimum. Here's a floor-to-ceiling collage that shows that you can be unconventional and balanced, too. On one half, a grid of black-and-white shots forms a powerful block of dark/light contrasts and imitates the pattern of the brick. The other half makes the switch to 3-D and color, with intense variations of shape and scale. Slide the yin and yang halves together and stand back: instant equilibrium.

Who can resist a do-it-yourself

undertaking that features steps like these:

1 Set something down wherever the mood strikes you.

2 Relax for an hour, or a day, or a week.

3 The next time you find yourself carrying around something else that doesn't yet have a display spot, place it beside the first piece.

4 Continue repeating steps 1 through 3 for as long as you like.

One of the best ways to blend pictures and other pieces is to let the process become organic and ongoing. Add a new object on a whim. Pull another one out to see if you like the empty space it leaves. Just follow the clues of texture, color, shape, and, if you like, subject matter as you go. The display here seems to suggest that anything featuring rich wood, earth tones, or a touch of primitive flair is welcome.

OFF the WALL

SOME OF THE MOST POPULAR PLACES FOR PICTURES AREN'T WALLS AT ALL. They're the horizontal surfaces—mantels, pianos, end tables, shelves, windowsills, and so on—where we set up standing displays. To give yours more interest, vary the height of the pieces. Small picture stands and pedestals are sold for just this purpose. You can also use everything from pedestal cake stands and painted bricks to glass blocks and decorative wooden boxes to add levels to a flat display.

at home with pictures

Charmingly random displays that look as if they were accidently (and effortlessly) tossed together seldom were. In this casual mix, for example, the subject of vessels repeats itself in similar colors, ranging from clear to cool grays and blues. In addition, various pieces appear to point to each other—the spout on the seltzer bottle down to the model ship, and the brushes up to the pitcher in the painting—creating implied lines that invite viewers to fill in what's missing.

The objects that compose this still life on a mantel have nothing in common other than line and shape—and yet they combine to form a compelling display. The reed-thin candlesticks almost perfectly mimic the vertical lines of the pen-and-ink picture of the H. In contrast, the two long necks of the vases on the other end offer more of a hint at the form. Even more subtle, but helping everything connect, the rounded piles of rocks roughly echo the bottoms of the vases.

at home with pictures

OFF
the WALL

HERE'S AN IDEA FOR THE WHY-MAKE-THIS-HARDER-THAN-IT-HAS-TO-BE CATEGORY. Use streamlined office clips, great big bulldog clips, colored clothespins, even kitschy hair clips to fasten a few unframed photos to a lamp, mirror, visor, headboard, or some other everyday spot.

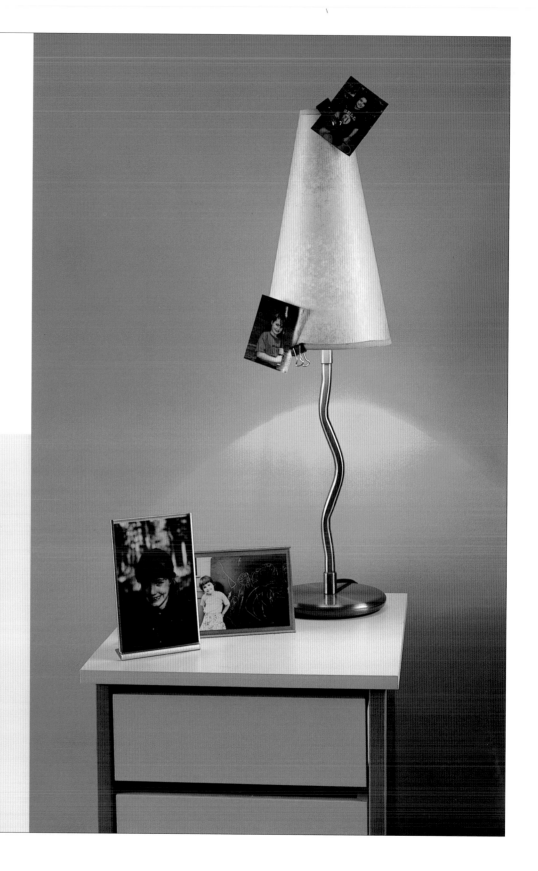

Sometimes, even the faintest connection can effectively link together a group of disparate pictures and other pieces. This unusual collection of textured paintings, weathered wood, ceramic fragments, and natural objects is held together by its narrow range of complementary colors—all brownish-orange and bluish-gray. Together, they form a color scheme that might suit a winter landscape. The quiet blend helps the objects hang together as a whole.

Use screw eyes to string a wire from one side of an empty picture frame to the other; then use clips and hooks of various kinds to hang pieces from the wire.

problem
solving

problem: A special note from your sister, the tiny card that came with a bouquet of flowers, a small newspaper clipping that lists your son's name on the school honor roll. What if you want to display it, but it doesn't seem like frameable, mountable art?

solution: Here are three inventive ways to capture and display all those little bits of ephemera, along with the postcards, snapshots, and other pictures that go with them.

Buy some decorative, no-roll elastic (sold with sewing notions), and tack or staple two strips to the back of a picture frame, so the strips cross in the opening on the front in an X shape. Cover the frame's backing with fabric. Tuck your display items snugly in place under the elastic strips.

Fill a picture frame with a piece of plain or decorative paper, then use glue to attach little pockets (sold with scrapbooking supplies) to the paper. Slip the pieces you want to show off into the slots.

Matching styles is one of the best ways to blend pictures with the other pieces in a setting. Hang a series of black-and-white cityscapes in sleek black frames over this folksy set of coat hooks, and it simply wouldn't work. The barn-wood frames held together with worn hinges, on the other hand, are perfectly at home.

PERSONALIZING YOUR HOOKS WITH PICTURES

Maybe you're among the many who have resorted to a row of coat hooks or a section of cubbies near a frequently used door to corral the jackets, caps, shoes, keys, and dog leashes that make their way in and out. To give your storage spot a dash of style and personality, code each hook or cubby hole by hanging a small photo of its user above it. You can even personalize the frames, depending on whether the photo features a soccer player, carpool driver, or Frisbee–catching pooch.

You don't have to come up with an elaborate montage to join pictures with other elements in a meaningful way. Something as simple as this mat with double openings can be all you need to tell a complete visual story. Here, it unites an old family photo of two sisters with a letter from one to the other. You could use the same format to display a birth announcement with a baby photo, a travel shot with a postcard home, maybe even a piece of your creative writing from elementary school alongside a photo of you receiving your college diploma.

Alternating picture, object, picture, object can be a perfect approach—especially when your subject matter is as classic as these traditional fruit paintings and lids from porcelain soup tureens. Plate hangers, which use spring-loaded tension to grip the edges of a piece from the back, are the most secure way to hang lids, saucers, platters, and other similarly shaped dishes.

Teaming display cases with pictures

is an especially orderly way to incorporate other objects into the mix. The rectangular boxes in the photo above slip right into place beside an extremely unified collection of frames. The pairing suggests a relationship between their contents—old architectural tools—and the drawings of the columns. The display's photographs, on the other hand, blend in, not because of their subject matter, but with the help of their neutral-tone frames. In the photo on the right, the display case acts as both anchor and shelf. The picture and other pieces of cowboy paraphernalia seem to revolve around the hub the box provides.

objects as art

E ven if you don't own walls full of original paintings, and professional photographs, chances are that you *are* surrounded by a rich supply of the evidence of what you've done, where you've gone, and how you spend your time. Whether that evidence includes seed packets for spring flowers, a stack of subway tokens, pages of sheet music, or a box of campaign buttons, it's meaningful because it represents your memories, your pastimes, your daily life, and your passions.

It's probably also pretty interesting to look at. Frame pieces of it; showcase others in shadow boxes; hang some from hooks and display rods; and glue, wire, or otherwise attach the rest to various backings. In the process, the ordinary artifacts of your life suddenly become objects of one-of-a-kind art.

textiles

- Handwoven rugs
- An heirloom quilt
- Scraps of silk, all in separate small gold frames
- Your grandmother's monogrammed lace napkins
- Baby blankets on a nursery wall
- Panels of African mud cloth or brilliant-colored molas

sticks, stones, and other natural objects

- Fall leaves floated between two sheets of glass
- A shadow box with multiple, same-size compartments, each filled with a different river stone
- A long row of a dozen dried roses
- Cattails attached to a piece of backing with twine
- A display of dried seed pods all tacked to a mat
- Small bundles of twigs

collections and memorabilia

- The tiny pieces of dollhouse furniture you've saved since you were seven
- Costume jewelry
- Album covers
- Scraps of wallpaper stripped off the walls of your grandparents' old farmhouse
- Hand mirrors
- Small pieces of beach glass glued to a mirrored backing

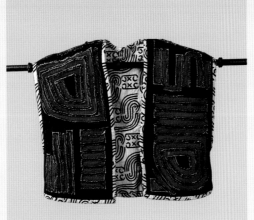

printed pieces

- Wedding, baby, and graduation announcements
- Diplomas
- Handmade wrapping paper
- Pages from a 19th-century gardening book
- Greeting cards
- Old journal pages, shop ledgers, or pages of handwritten school papers

clothing

- Headdresses, belts, or other pieces of ceremonial clothing or accessories from another culture
- All the bright-colored single socks you knitted as practice pieces
- Embroidered labels from vintage clothing shown off in small, wide-matted frames
- Baby shoes
- Beaded scarves
- A series of bow ties lined up in a long, vertical frame

the ordinary but visually interesting

- Unusual buttons sewn onto a fabric-covered mat
- A row of black sunglasses
- Wooden spoons
- Corks from wine bottles wired to a piece of backing
- Unsharpened yellow pencils
- Chopsticks displayed in a fan-shaped arrangement

Shadow boxes are essentially deep–backed frames that make it easy to display all sorts of three-dimensional objects. Some come equipped with lots of compartments, perfect for sectioning off small pieces of a collection. Others have display shelves. These customized, glass-front shadow boxes, fashioned out of old drawers, make a study of the shapes and textures of cranberries, rose petals, and dried herbs. The simple square boxes on the next page come with grooves in the bottom that help hold this family of plates in place, and the open fronts make it easy to change to a different color scheme or style or a new object altogether when the mood strikes.

IT could be a page from the day when you purchased your first stock. It could represent what you do for a living. Or, it could be a commentary on what the stock page is to you: a graphically pleasing series of black-and-white bars suitable for framing and displaying in your living room. Whichever, it makes an original and easy-to-come-by presentation.

Other ordinary printed pieces that could easily make the switch to display piece:

- Cash register receipts

- A page from a dictionary or manual

- Invoices with interesting logos

- Flight itineraries

- A page of computer code

- A bar graph or pie chart

- A page of personal ads

- An index to an atlas

Salvaging architectural details from old buildings and homes—every thing from French doors to wooden newel posts—and incorporating them into contemporary designs is a decorating trend that's taken hold. One of the easiest ways to dip into it is to turn interesting bits of recycled infrastructure into hanging art. Here, a decorative piece from a building facade adds texture to its sleek new setting.

Other salvaged details you might want to have hanging around:

- Ceiling tiles
- Shutters
- Register grates
- Glass doorknobs
- Window panes
- A collection of hinges
- Detail from an iron gate
- Decorative shelf brackets
- Porcelain faucet knobs

at home with pictures

**DESKTOP PICTURE HOLDERS THAT CLASP INDIVIDUAL PHOTOS
IN THEIR WIRE ARMS** and fan them out in a display are available
nowadays everywhere frames are sold. Salvaged and found
objects can perform the same task, but provide a more original
look. Here, we've used old bill holders. For a weathered-wood
option, prop up a shutter and stick your pictures in its slots.

OFF
the WALL

Ever since hieroglyphic panels were unearthed from ancient Egyptian tombs,

we've been intrigued with the symbols that make up writing systems. Why not let your best friend's distinctively curly y's or your favorite uncle's unmistakable all-caps printing serve as their own pieces worthy of study and appreciation? In the simplest of styles, this handwritten letter, along with a few pressed pansies, is floated between pieces of plastic sheeting held together with binder clips. If you wanted to add to the airy effect, you could layer in transparent sheets of colored paper, then hang the pieces in front of a window with monofilament fishing line.

These
pictureless frames-
turned-shelves make artful
display pieces. Pick up a
few empty wooden frames
for a song at a tag sale or
flea market. Spruce them up
with fresh paint; add some
reinforcing molding to the back;
and nail small, light precut
shelves (available at home
improvement centers) in place
along the inside bottom edges.

problem
solving

problem: You have absolutely nothing you think is interesting and attractive enough to hang on your walls.

solution: Think again—and take a look at what an effective display these ultrautilitarian objects make. To create an arrangement with this sort of impact, choose pieces that blend well with your color scheme and create a rhythmic pattern. And don't underestimate the I-never-would-have-thought-of-that appeal of celebrating the lines and shapes of objects as ordinary as these four rulers and half-a-dozen small jewelry envelopes.

Curating your own collection, whether it's of fishing lures, harmonicas, antique game boards, or keys, is an art form in itself. You study. You search. You embrace some pieces. You edit others out. And you end up with a visual record of what you take delight in. Go ahead and carry your personal expression to the next level by hanging your unique body of work on the wall.

138

GO ahead. Let the trend watchers tell us that minimalism is over, that the backlash against "less is more" has everyone now piling it on. Some of us will forever cling to a spare style in which typed stanzas of poetry on a page give us all the shape and movement we need from a piece of wall art. This pared-down alternative to traditional pictures even features an unadorned hanging mechanism: double-sided tape.

From hand-dyed tapestries to woven panels, textiles have long been popular wall hangings. In the days before central heat, they helped insulate drafty rooms. Now, they're simply another way to add color, texture, and design to your walls. These two very different examples start with the common theme of quilts, then take the idea in opposite directions. Set off in a weathered frame, the delicate antique remnant below assumes a place of honor amid other heirlooms. The lively painted-fabric quilt on the right, on the other hand, is stretched over a frame and tacked in place to energize a modern setting.

HANGING RUGS

One of the easiest ways to hang a rug without damaging it is to use a strip of carpet tacks. Cut the strip to the width of the rug with a saw or a pair of ratchet pruners. Slip on some protective gloves, use a level to line your strip up straight, and screw it to the wall at the point where the rug will hang. If the rug is extremely heavy, use anchor bolts or toggle bolts to attach the strip to the wall. Be sure the tacks are pointing upward. Press the rug against the tacks, which will hold it firmly on the carpet strip.

breaking
the and
rules getting away
with it

C over no more than
two-thirds of
a blank wall with hanging
pieces, say the experts who issue
guidelines about such subjects. Here,
we imagine their next, unspoken bit of
advice: *But if you're going to rebel, go all
the way.* The variety of frame sizes and
shapes gives this mirror-covered wall
some breathing room, so it feels full
but not overloaded. In addition, all
the reflective surfaces add an overall
sense of spaciousness.

These long, tall calligraphy panels could very well have decorated the home of the person who once wore the framed robe. They also establish a color sequence that the garment repeats, while both blend in tone with the Asian painting in the room beyond.

FRAMING AND DISPLAYING CLOTHING

If you want to turn a whole item of clothing—a christening dress, a tribal outfit, an embroidered jacket—into a hanging display that's encased, you probably need to visit a custom framer. A display case is the best option for large items. Your framer can help you decide whether the garment should be secured to a piece of backing or suspended on a rod. If you have a clothing piece you don't feel needs the protection of a case, slide it onto a curtain rod, and hang the rod from two hooks.

KEEPSAKE BOXES, JOURNAL COVERS, JEWELRY BOXES, EVEN BACKPACKS AND SHOULDER BAGS now come in designs that include slots for slipping in small pictures. They offer an interesting way for your pictures to migrate off the walls and onto coffee tables, nightstands, bureaus—and even out into the world with you.

OFF
the WALL

contributors

STEVEN AIMONE, who earned his MFA at Brooklyn College, is a visual composer, arts educator, and independent curator based in Asheville, North Carolina. His paintings and collage works have been the subject of exhibitions in New York City, London, Florida, and North Carolina. He has served as Visiting Instructor of Art at both Western Carolina University and Stetson University, and also as Artistic Director of a large commercial gallery in New Smyrna Beach, Florida, called Arts on Douglas. Steve has taught numerous workshops in composition and color through ProArt Institute, a non-profit "university without walls" based in Ormond Beach, Florida. He is currently writing a book on design for Lark Books, scheduled for publication in 2003. Steve consulted on the content of *At Home with Pictures*.

TERRY TAYLOR lives and works in Asheville, North Carolina, as an editor and project coordinator for Lark Books. He is a prolific designer and exhibiting artist, and works in media ranging from metals and jewelry to paper crafts and mosaics. Some of the most recent Lark books to which he has contributed include *Creative Outdoor Lighting, Salvage Style,* and *The Book of Wizard Craft.* Terry created a number of the displays featured throughout the book.

a note about suppliers

Usually, the supplies you need for making the projects in Lark books can be found at your local craft supply store, discount mart, home improvement center, or retail shop relevant to the topic of the book. Occasionally, however, you may need to buy materials or tools from specialty suppliers. In order to provide you with the most up-to-date information, we have created a list of suppliers on our Web site, which we update on a regular basis. Visit us at www.larkbooks.com, click on "Craft Supply Sources," and then click on the relevant topic. You will find numerous companies listed with their web address and/or mailing address and phone number.

index